AUSTRALIAN BICENTENNIAL
COLLECTION

1788-1988

AUSTRALIAN BICENTENNIAL COLLECTION
Book 1 *The First Australians*
Book 2 *Navigators and Shipwrecks*
Book 3 *Botany Bay*
Book 4 *The First Fleet*

ILLUSTRATIONS:
Cover: Arthur Phillip, by Francis Wheatley
This page and title page: The Thames at Deptford

THE FIRST FLEET
Australia's heritage in stamps

Australia Post

Compiled by Jo Monie, Australia Post Stamps and Philatelic Branch
Designed by Sandra Baker, Australia Post Graphic Design Studio
© Australia Post 1987
Typesetters: Typographical Services, Melbourne
Colour separators: Enticott Polygraph, Melbourne
Printer: Cambec Press, Melbourne
ISBN 0 642 11946 5

Contents

Entrance of Rio de Janeiro (Raper)

The Voyage of The First Fleet

INTRODUCTION

For most of the people aboard the First Fleet, the voyage in 1787 to found a penal settlement in New South Wales was a journey to the end of the earth. Eleven ships sailed from England to Australia, under the command of Arthur Phillip in the flagship *HMS Sirius*.

The remainder of the Fleet was made up of the armed tender *HMS Supply*, six transport ships carrying convicts, and three storeships. In addition to provisions, stores and equipment, the Fleet carried some 1350 people.

The Fleet weighed anchor from Motherbank or Spithead near Portsmouth on 13 May 1787. The voyage of over 24,000 km was accomplished in 252 days, 68 of which were spent at ports en route: Teneriffe, Rio de Janeiro and Cape Town.

Botany Bay, the intended destination, proved unsuitable as a site for permanent settlement. With several of his officers, Governor Phillip took three rowing boats to Port Jackson where he found *"one of the finest harbours in the world."* On the evening of 26 January 1788 the British flag was raised on shore, and the King's health toasted. This simple ceremony at the end of the journey is regarded as the founding of the colony of New South Wales, and hence of the Australian nation.

Previous books in this series pay tribute to our Aboriginal heritage, *The First Australians;* describe early European exploration of the coastline, *Navigators and Shipwrecks;* and focus upon the momentous decision by the British Government to establish a penal colony at *Botany Bay*. The final book will outline the early years of settlement of New South Wales.

PEOPLE OF THE FIRST FLEET

In October 1786, soon after the British Government decided to establish a penal colony in New South Wales, the appointment was announced of Captain Arthur Phillip, of the Royal Navy, as Commander of the expedition and Governor of the new colony. Captain John Hunter and other naval officers serving under Phillip were responsible for ensuring a safe journey and for the general administration of the Fleet. To guard the convicts a Marine Corps was raised under the command of Major Robert Ross.

It is thought that about 760 convicts sailed aboard the crowded transport ships with twenty-four of their children. They were guarded by about 240 marines, accompanied by some thirty wives and twenty children. The remaining 300 people were mainly naval officers and crew. merchant seamen and officials.

Convicts embarking for Botany Bay (Rowlandson)

Fascinating vignettes of First Fleet life can be found in the surviving journals and letters written during the voyage. Among the published accounts are the diaries of naval officers John Hunter, Philip Gidley King and William Bradley, naval surgeon John White, marine officers Watkin Tench and Ralph Clark, marine soldiers James Scott and John Easty and civilian surgeon Arthur Bowes Smyth. The version attributed to Arthur Phillip was in fact compiled by others from Phillip's papers, although his original letters have survived. Also of interest are David Collins' two volume memoir, and the letters of midshipman Daniel Southwell. The manuscripts of these accounts have been transcribed to convey as closely as possible the content of the original handwriting.

It is worth bearing in mind that the diaries reflect the preoccupations of the writers: tides and map readings loom large in King's journal; his wife Betsy in that of homesick Ralph Clark; the health of the convicts and marines in the surgeons' accounts. We lack any direct contemporary insight into the feelings of the convicts, and most particularly there is no diary written by a woman.

Arthur Phillip   Philip Gidley King   John Hunter   David Collins   Watkin Tench

THE SHIPS

HMS Sirius, the flagship, was built for the East India trade, but caught fire when first loaded and burnt to the water-line. The hull was then bought by the Admiralty, and rebuilt in 1781. Named the *Berwick*, she made two voyages to the West Indies carrying stores. In October 1786 the *Berwick* was recommissioned under Phillip's command and her name changed to *Sirius*, a bright star in the southern skies. Travelling on the *Sirius* were 160 naval officers and men, including Phillip, Hunter, King and Bradley.

It is thought that *HMS Supply* was built in 1759, but little is known of her early history. She was commissioned in October 1786 as an armed tender, under the command of Lieutenant Henry Lidgbird Ball, RN. A brig-rigged sloop and the smallest ship of the Fleet, the *Supply* carried a complement of 50 seamen.

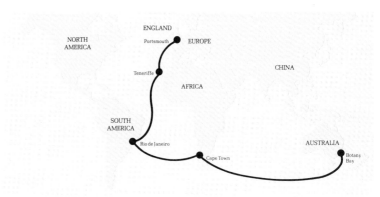

Cape of Good Hope (Raper)

The six convict transports were commercial vessels hired for the voyage, manned by merchant seamen, and, with the exception of the *Friendship*, all were fully square-rigged with three masts. The largest was the *Alexander*, a little over 114 feet (34.8m) carrying 195 male convicts. The two newest ships carried the majority of the convict women: *Lady Penrhyn*, with 101 prisoners; and the *Prince of Wales*, with forty-nine female and one male convict. Comparable in size with these two was the *Charlotte*, a barque of 105 feet (32m) with eighty-eight male and twenty female convicts.

Marine commander Major Ross travelled on the *Scarborough*, together with a large marine detachment and 209 male convicts. The smallest transport was the *Friendship*, a brig, carrying seventy-four male and twenty-one female convicts.

The balance of the Fleet comprised the three storeships: *Fishburn*, *Golden Grove* and *Borrowdale*.

THE ROUTE

The circuitous route followed by the First Fleet, from the Canary Islands across the Atlantic ocean to Rio de Janeiro in Brazil, then back across the southern Atlantic to the Cape of Good Hope, was dictated by wind considerations, especially the frequent calm spells experienced near the African coast.

All twenty-one First Fleet stamps, when placed in sequence, form a continuous image of the voyage and ports of call. The issue dates are the bicentenaries of the dates upon which the Fleet departed from Portsmouth, arrived at Teneriffe, Rio de Janeiro and Cape Town, and landed at Sydney Cove.

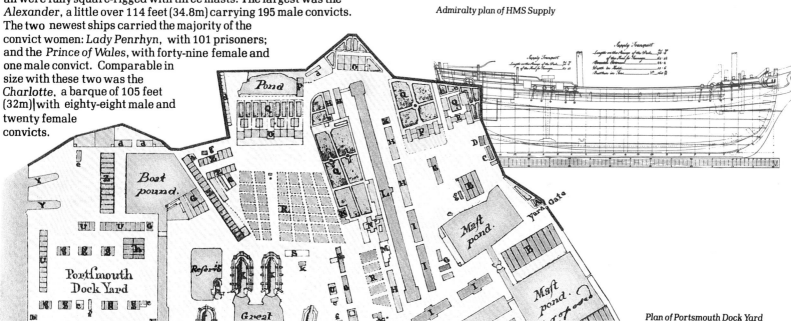

Admiralty plan of HMS Supply

Plan of Portsmouth Dock Yard

Departure

"In general the Convicts have behaved well, I saw them all yesterday, for the first time, they are quiet and contented. Tho' there are amongst them, some compleat Villains"

wrote Arthur Phillip to Evan Nepean, Under Secretary of State.

The convicts were taken from gaols and hulks around the country and loaded aboard the ships, either at dockyards along the Thames or at Portsmouth, where the Fleet was finally assembled. By the time that the Fleet departed, large numbers of prisoners had already been aboard ship for several months.

On arrival at Portsmouth, some convicts were in very poor health, and many of the women were, in Phillip's words:

"... almost naked, & so very filthy, that nothing but Cloathing them could have prevented them from perishing ..."

Crimes then punishable by transportation ranged from petty theft and forgery to armed robbery and assault.

Convicts near Blackfriars Bridge

'Portsmouth Point' (Rowlandson)

Departure

A party of marines was raised to travel with the Fleet to Botany Bay:

"... not only to enforce due subordination and obedience in the Settlement intended to be formed there, but for the Defence of the Settlement against the incursion of the Natives ..."

Marines were naval soldiers, and their selection as troops for the New South Wales settlement concentrated bureaucratic activity with the Admiralty. Also, as Captain Watkin Tench explained:

"Had a regiment recruited since the war been sent out, sea-sickness would have incapacitated half the men from performing the duties immediately and indispensably necessary; whereas the marines, from being accustomed to serve on board ship, accommodated themselves with ease to every exigency, and surmounted every difficulty."

The marines supplied several of the new colony's officials, notably Major Robert Ross, who was commissioned Lieutenant Governor, and Captain David Collins, Deputy Judge Advocate. Collins was later Lieutenant Governor of the abortive settlement near Sorrento, and subsequently of the Van Diemen's Land colony. Lieutenant William Dawes, a competent astronomer, was employed as engineer and surveyor of the New South Wales settlement, and Lieutenant George Johnston was later prominent in the mutiny against Governor Bligh.

Several of the marines wrote plaintively to Lord Sydney in November 1786:

"We beg leave to propose, that the wives of the Marines going to Botany Bay, not exceeding ten to each Company, which will not in the whole amount to more than Forty women, may be allowed to embark with them."

About thirty wives of marines are thought to have sailed with the Fleet, some with children. Officers' wives were not permitted, however, much to the chagrin of Lieutenant Ralph Clark, who did his utmost to get his adored wife and child aboard the *Friendship*.

Morning promenade

Seamen and boat (Atkinson)

Departure

Originally, the Government intended that the Fleet should sail by the end of 1786, but this proved to be impossible. Ships had to be found and refitted, the convicts assembled, officers, troops and crew selected and outfitted, and supplies bought and loaded. Everything required for a colony of several hundred people had to be taken aboard the ships, as the line of supply from England could not be guaranteed, and it would take months, if not years, for the colonists to begin producing food crops.

Loaded at Portsmouth, supplemented by items acquired at ports of call along the way, were clothes, food and drink, wood for fires, tools and utensils, building materials, furnishings, horses, cattle, sheep, pigs, dogs, poultry, food for the animals, medical supplies, weapons and ammunition, plants and seeds, books and papers, bedding, and everything else necessary for the colony's survival. One of the surgeons even took his piano, and entertained his fellow officers after dinner on board ship.

By March 1787, Phillip was urging that arrangements be expedited:

"Fresh Meat for all the Convicts, and Wine for the Sick I was informed had been ordered, in consequence of the representation I made as soon as the Ships got round to Portsmouth–but the Sick only, have Fresh Meat. Wine at the discretion of the Surgeon is very necessary for the Sick ...

The giving Cloaths to those Convicts who have been Embarked at Plymouth, is so very necessary, that I have ordered it to be done ...

Let me repeat my desire that orders may be immediately be given to increase the Convicts allowance of Bread. 16 Pounds of Bread for 42 days is very little."

Convicts at work

Two seamen (Atkinson)

The Thames at Deptford

Departure

Both the *Sirius* and *Supply* and the six transports were fitted out at Deptford Docks before the voyage to Australia. All eleven ships were assembled at Portsmouth in March, but another two months were to elapse before departure. The background in the first four stamps is a composite of the dockyards on the Thames, and of Portsmouth.

Conditions on board the *Alexander*, in particular, were most insanitary. The loading of convicts on the *Alexander* and *Lady Penrhyn* had commenced at Woolwich early in January, and by 15 April eleven men had died on the *Alexander* and one woman on the *Lady Penrhyn*. Convicts were removed from the *Alexander* while it was thoroughly scoured, but another five deaths occurred before sailing. The health of the convicts improved en route, attributed to a combination of generous food rations, conscientious medical care, and insistence on cleanliness as far as that was possible in the conditions below deck.

Deptford Docks (Cleveley)

Rumours of a malignant disease rampant among the Fleet before departure were quashed by Surgeon General John White, who firmly stated *"that the whole fleet was in as good a state of health, and as few in it would be found to be ill, at that cold season of the year, as even in the most healthy situation on shore."*

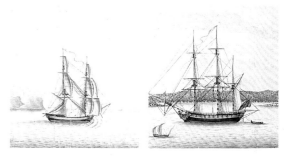

HMS Supply   HMS Sirius

Departure

Inclement weather contributed to the delayed departure of the Fleet, already hampered by problems, especially supply shortages. Phillip did not receive his formal Commission as Captain General and Governor in Chief of the Territory of New South Wales until the end of April 1787. He had remained in London, attending to administrative details, and joined the Sirius at Portsmouth in May.

A last minute delay occurred in a dispute concerning the pay of the merchant seamen. As Lieutenant King explained:

"They had been in employ upwards of seven Months, during which time they had received no pay except their River pay & one Months advance. The great length of the Voyage rendered it necessary that they should have more Mony, to furnish themselves with such necessarys as were really indispensable. But it became the Masters interest to withhold their pay from them, that they might be obliged to purchase those necessarys from them on ye course of the Voyage at a very exorbitant rate."

Phillip finally abandoned waiting for all the supplies to arrive, and gave the order for the Fleet to sail in the early morning of Sunday 13 May 1787. The logbook of the Sirius recorded the event:

"... at 4 AM fired a Gun and made the Signal to weigh, weigh'd and made sail, in Company with the Hyaena Frigate, Supply Armed Tender, Six Transports and Three Store Ships, at 9 fired a Gun and made the Sig'l for the Convoy to make more sail."

Sirius, Supply and Convoy passing the Needles (Bradley)

By 10 am the Fleet had cleared the Isle of Wight, and Tench strolled among the convicts, observing their demeanour:

"A very few excepted, their countenances indicated a high degree of satisfaction, though in some, the pang of being severed, perhaps for ever, from their native land, could not be wholly suppressed; in general, marks of distress were more perceptible among the men than the women ..."

For the first week, as the Fleet sailed down the English Channel and into open waters, it was escorted by the naval frigate HMS Hyaena. The convicts were released from their irons to make them more comfortable, although this action increased the risk of uprisings. One such attempt was quickly suppressed aboard the Scarborough, and the ringleaders punished.

View of the Needles, Isle of Wight (Raper)

Teneriffe

Strong winds were encountered as the Fleet headed for Teneriffe, in the Canary Islands, the first port of call. Teneriffe is spelt here according to eighteenth century usage; the modern Anglicised spelling is Tenerife.

Damage caused by the heavy seas was noted by Surgeon Arthur Bowes Smyth:

"A 4 p.m. the Supply Brig carried away her Main Top Gallt. Mast—a great swell. Kill'd a pig—The Commodore sent the Supply Brig ahead to look out for land. The Friendship carried away her main top Galt. Mast."

The *Supply*, the swiftest ship in the Fleet, was frequently used to carry messages and to go ahead to watch out for land.

On board the *Sirius*, Phillip requested that information be compiled concerning the convicts, and Bowes Smyth mentioned that this work was in progress.

"... A Boat from the Fishburn, (The Agent's Ship) to desire a List of the Convicts, with their Crimes, time of Tryal & the term of their Transportation."

Several of the diarists recorded the wildlife observed en route, including sharks, albatrosses, and many porpoises. Pictured on the stamp is the common dolphin, with its characteristic yellow patch.

The *Supply* signalled that land had been sighted on 29 May, and the next day the Fleet passed the Deserters, a group of rocks off Madeira. Another rocky cluster, the Salvages, came into view, followed at last by Teneriffe, their first landfall.

The First Fleet's route from England to the Equator, through the Canary Islands—dotted line on right (Bradley)

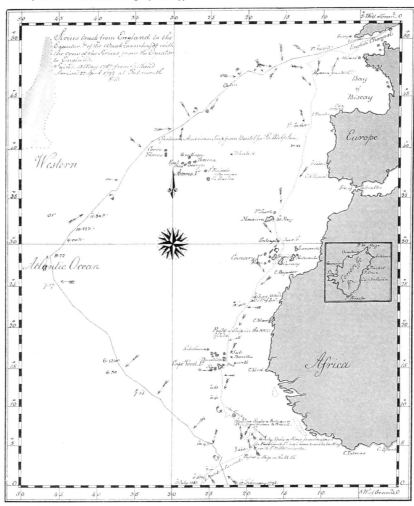

Teneriffe

On 3 June 1787, three weeks after leaving England, the Fleet arrived at Teneriffe, renowned for its spectacular mountain peak.

Spain's Governor of the Canaries, the Marquis de Brancifort, greeted the Fleet respectfully and entertained Phillip and his senior officers ashore. Watkin Tench was most impressed:

"During our short stay we had every day some fresh proof of his Excellency's esteem and attention, and had the honour of dining with him, in a style of equal elegance and splendour. At this entertainment the profusion of ices which appeared in the desert was surprising, considering that we were enjoying them under a sun nearly vertical. But it seems the caverns of the Peak, very far below its summit, afford, at all seasons, ice in abundance."

The Fleet called at Teneriffe to replenish supplies of water and vegetables. Taking on fresh water occupied several days, as each water barrel had to be filled ashore and then ferried out to the ships in small boats. Vegetables were in short supply, but pumpkins, onions, figs and mulberries were procured. While in port the marines, sailors and convicts alike received fresh meat, fruit and vegetables.

Phillip lost no time in writing to Lord Sydney:

"By the inclosed list Your Lordship will see that the Convicts are not so Sickly as when we Sailed, and while we remain here the Commissary will be able to procure them Fresh Meat, at a very moderate expence.

I understood when the Marines who were to form the Garrison were Embarked, that they would be furnished with Ammunition, but since we sailed, find that they were only supplied with what was necessary for immediate service, while in Port ...

I am therefore to request that Your Lordship will be pleased to give Orders, that those Articles may be sent out by the First Ship, and for which, as well as for the Womens Cloathing, that was left behind, we shall be much distressed."

Opinions of the town of Santa Cruz varied. Bowes Smyth thought it *"rather a mean Town,"* while Watkin Tench was moderate in his praise:

"... its cheerful white appearance, contrasted with the dreary brownness of the back ground, makes not an unpleasing coup d'oeil. It is neither irregular in its plan, nor despicable in its style of building; and the churches and religious houses are numerous, sumptuous, and highly ornamented."

On 7 June the town celebrated the Festival of Corpus Christi and some of the officers went ashore to watch the proceedings. Lt William Bradley wrote that the Festival was *"announced early in the morning by ringing the Bells of all the Convents, Monasteries & Churches in the Town."*

Peak of Teneriffe and town of Santa Cruz

Santa Cruz, in the Island of Teneriffe.

Teneriffe

The local people fished among the ships of the Fleet, and the people aboard the Fleet caught fish at every opportunity to supplement their rations. Bonito, caught in the nets on the stamp, resembles the bluefin tuna.

During the week at Teneriffe, King and others formed a party to visit Laguna, the island's capital. They set off at 8 am, accompanied by *"numerous attendants, whose principal business it was to accelerate ye nature of the Cavalry, by means of long staffs pointed with Iron, & with which they also leaped with surprizing agility from rock to rock."*

The harvest was in progress as they travelled through *"a very pleasant picturesque country"* to Laguna, *"a very unwholesome place"* set on a poorly drained marsh. The party returned that evening *"much amuzed on ye Road with the singing & mirth of our Sunburnt guides."*

A fight broke out on shore between sailors from a visiting Dutch East Indiaman and the *Sirius* crew, resulting, according to Bowes Smyth, in *"some broken pates & bloody noses."* On the same night a convict escaped:

"One of the Convicts on board the Alexr. ... Escaped by getting out at the Stern into the Jolly Boat, wt. which he went off unperceived, but upon a party being sent out next morng. along shore to look after him he was discover'd abt. 6 leagues off asleep on the shore wt. the Boat lying among the rocks ..."

Santa Cruz

John Powers, the convict, was recaptured on 9 June, and the following morning the Fleet set sail, bound for Rio de Janeiro. The view of the Peak as the Fleet moved away from the island was much admired by Tench:

"In sailing from Teneriffe to the south-east, the various and picturesque appearances of the Peak are beautiful to the highest degree. The stupendous height, which before was lost on the traveller, now strikes him with awe and admiration, the whole island appearing one vast mountain with a pyramidal top."

Santa Cruz on the SE side of Teneriffe: Sirius & Convoy in the Roads (Bradley)

Rio de Janeiro

The journey from Teneriffe to Rio de Janeiro took eight weeks, in the course of which the Fleet crossed the Tropic of Cancer. Sergeant Scott described the festivities:

"... the Usual Seremoney Was perform^d, With those that had Not Cross^d. the Line before,–Which Was Ducking Lathering With tar Grase &^c and Shav^d. N.B. the Seamen perform^d this Seremony ..."

Similar rites marked the crossing of the Equator.

HMS Supply (Marquardt)

Phillip had originally intended calling in at the Cape Verde Islands, but *"the want of favourable wind, and the opposition of a strong current"* caused a change of plan, to general disappointment. Stops en route were a welcome diversion after the long weeks on board ship.

Winds were variable, with stormy seas at times making life most uncomfortable. *"The Squalls continue very frequently & the Ship often lyes down so much we can scarcely keep our seats at table"* wrote Arthur Bowes Smyth.

The same diarist was most impressed by a whale, which he estimated to be the same length as the ship on which he was travelling, the 31.7 metre *Lady Penrhyn*:

"Abt. 12 o'Clock at noon a very large Whale rose abt. 20 Yards from the Ship's side, & blow'd the water very high wt. a great noise. I was standing on the poop with Capt. Sever & looking directly at the spot in wh. it arose & being the first Whale I had ever seen it startled me not a little. it was full as long as the Ship, spouted the water several times, swam majestically along by the Ship's side, cross'd the stern, blow'd & went down head foremost & it(s) enormous tail a great heighth out of the water.

Other marine life seen in the passage across the Atlantic include flying fish, sharks and dolphins.

Land was sighted on 2 August, signalled by the *Supply*. Calm spells delayed their approach, and it was not until 6 August that the Fleet was anchored in the harbour.

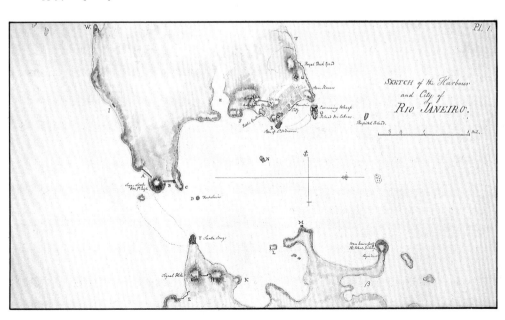

Rio de Janeiro

Rio de Janeiro, also known then as St Sebastian, was the capital of Brazil. The city's wealth was founded on the diamond mines discovered nearby in 1730. The picturesque harbour was defended by forts, with *"a hill shaped like a sugar loaf"* on the west side.

Earlier in his career Phillip had served in the Portuguese navy, and his reception in Rio de Janeiro, a Portuguese port, attested to the high regard in which he was still held. A thirteen gun salute marked the arrival of the Fleet. Both Phillip and his officers were received with great courtesy by the Governor of Brazil, known as the Viceroy, and unusual privileges were extended including permission to visit all parts of the city and to make short excursions into the country.

Bowes Smyth reported that several officers enjoyed drinking tea in an orange grove near the shore:

"... within less than 100 yards of the Beach they were surrounded by Orange, Lemon & Lime Trees, also Indigo, Pine Apples & many other kinds of plants & fruits all wh. they may have for the gathering. There were also great numbers of birds & enormous Butterflies, both extremely beautiful of their kind ..."

Canoes rowed by negro slaves moved among the ships of the Fleet, selling fruit and other fresh food. Thomas Barrett, a convict, managed to pass counterfeit coins to these traders, to Surgeon John White's grudging admiration. The coins had been made from buckles, buttons and pewter spoons during the voyage from Teneriffe.

"The impression, milling, character, in a word, the whole was so inimitably executed that had their metal been a little better the fraud, I am convinced, would have passed undetected. A strict and careful search was made for the apparatus wherewith this was done, but in vain; not the smallest trace or vestige of any thing of the kind was to be found among them. How they managed this business without discovery, or how they could effect it at all, is a matter of inexpressible surprise to me, as they never were suffered to come near a fire and a centinel was constantly placed over their hatchway, which, one would imagine, rendered it impossible for either fire or fused metal to be conveyed into their apartments. Besides, hardly ten minutes ever elapsed, without an officer of some degree or other going down among them."

View in Rio de Janeiro (Parkinson)

Fortified bay, Rio de Janeiro (Bradley)

Rio de Janeiro

The bustling markets offered a profusion of supplies, including cabbages, yams, bananas, guavas, limes, lettuces, oranges, pineapples, radishes, endive and beef. Several diarists noted the improved health of the convicts following increased allowances of fresh food, David Collins for example:

"... the convicts were each served daily with a pound of rice and a pound and an half of fresh meat (beef), together with a suitable proportion of vegetables. Great numbers of oranges were at different times distributed among them, and every possible care was taken to refresh and put them into a state of health and condition to resist the attacks of the scurvy, should it make its appearance in the long passage over the ocean which was yet between them and New South Wales."

During their four weeks in Rio de Janeiro, the naval officers and marines made frequent visits ashore, although Watkin Tench was disappointed by the ladies of the town:

"I must observe, that the custom of throwing nosegays at strangers, for the purpose of bringing on an assignation, which Doctor Solander, and another gentleman of Mr Cook's ship, met with when here, was never seen by any of us in a single instance. We were so deplorably unfortunate as to walk every evening before their windows and balconies, without being honoured with a single bouquet, though nymphs and flowers were in equal and great abundance."

Street singer (Debret)

Street scene (Debret)

Refreshment after lunch,
Rio de Janeiro (Debret)

Rio de Janeiro

Religious fervour was well in evidence in the streets of Rio de Janeiro, with numerous churches and convents, and frequent religious processions. According to Watkin Tench:

"... the height to which religious zeal is carried in this place, cannot fail of creating astonishment in a stranger. The greatest part of the inhabitants seem to have no other occupation, than that of paying visits and going to church ...

... From morning to night the ears of a stranger are greeted by the tinkling of the convent bells, and his eyes saluted by processions of devotees ..."

David Collins made an interesting observation:

"At a corner of almost every street in the town we observed a small altar, dedicated generally to the Virgin, and decorated with curtains and lamps. Before these altars, at the close of every evening, the negroes assembled to chant their vespers, kneeling together in long rows in the street. The policy of thus keeping the minds of so large a body, as that of the black people in this town, not only in constant employment, but in awe and subjection, by the almost perpetual exercise of religious worship, was too obvious to need a comment."

Religious procession, Rio de Janeiro (Debret)

Street musicians (Debret)

Rio de Janeiro

While in port, the ships were victualled with everything thought necessary at this juncture, including seeds and plants, rum, sugar, meat, fruit and vegetables, casava (a bread substitute), tobacco, ammunition, wood, and, of course, water. Repairs to ships were carried out, rigging mended, instruments tested, court martials held and punishments inflicted. James Baker, a marine, received two hundred lashes for endeavouring to pass one of the counterfeit coins made by the convicts.

Phillip was able to send several letters to the Colonial Office, describing the Fleet's reception by the Portuguese, victualling arrangements, and costs. He mentioned that the convicts had been allowed on deck during the day, and many of them at night also.

The convicts' spiritual welfare was attended to by the Reverend Mr Johnson, who held divine service on two of the transports every Sunday while in port. Mr Johnson also officiated following the birth of a baby to Jane Scott, wife of Marine Sergeant James Scott:

"... My Wife was Deleve^d of a Daughter at one OClock P.M. After being Ill 27 hours. The Reverent Mr Johnston Came On Board & Chrisned, My Child."

Fireworks were observed several times during the stay in Rio de Janeiro, especially on 21 August in honour of the birthday of the Prince of Brazil, when *"The day concluded wt Bonfires, brilliant illuminations & very good fireworks."*

On 5 September the Fleet set sail for the Cape of Good Hope. As a final mark of respect from Don Luis de Vasconcelos, the Viceroy of Brazil, a twenty-one gun salute was fired as they passed the Fort of Santa Cruz. The salute was returned by the *Sirius*, and the Fleet headed out to sea.

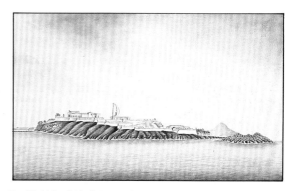

Fortified island, Rio de Janeiro (Raper)

Rio de Janeiro (Bradley)

Cape of Good Hope

During the five and a half week voyage across the southern Atlantic, light winds soon were succeeded by squalls and gales, causing damage to several of the ships. Rotten wood was found during an inspection of the *Sirius*, blamed by King on the *"extreem negligence"* of the dockyard officers in failing to carry out a proper inspection before the Fleet sailed from England. A mutiny attempt on the *Alexander* was quickly suppressed, and the offending seamen moved to another ship.

Land was sighted early in the morning of 13 October, and by dark the whole Fleet was anchored in Table Bay.

On board the *Lady Penrhyn*, Arthur Bowes Smyth surveyed the scene:

"Exactly 2 minutes before 6 o'Clock p.m. we drop'd Anchor in Table Bay, directly before Cape Town & the Table mountain. The face of the Country appears beautiful, the Town is back'd by very lofty Mountains many of wh. are cover'd wt. verdure, & great flocks of Sheep feeding thereon, particularly that called the Lyon's Rump. The Town is pretty large & appears to have many exceeding good houses in it. There are many Gallows & other impliments of punishment erected a long shore and in the front of the Town."

HMS Sirius and HMS Supply (Marquardt)

Map of Table Bay and Cape Town, early 1790s (Bridges)

Cape of Good Hope

Soon after arriving, Phillip visited the Dutch Governor, accompanied by Lieutenant King, to outline the Fleet's supply requirements, especially *"Cattle, Wine & Corn for y^e Voyage & bread for daily use"* (King). Cattle and wine presented no problem, but corn was already in short supply following a famine experienced over the past two years. Eventually all requests were agreed to, and provisions procured. In Phillip's words:

"... the ships, having on board not less than five hundred animals of different kinds, but chiefly poultry, put on an appearance which naturally enough excited the idea of Noah's ark."

The sheep acquired in Cape Town were remarkable for the very large size of their tails, which weighed between four and eight kilograms. The cattle are thought to have been Zebu, also known as Brahman, with their characteristic hump.

Tench described the livestock in more detail:

"The live animals we took on board on the public account from the Cape, for stocking our projected colony, were, two bulls, three cows, three horses, forty-four sheep, and thirty-two hogs, besides goats, and a very large quantity of poultry of every kind. A considerable addition to this was made by the private stocks of the officers, who were, however, under a necessity of circumscribing their original intentions on this head very much, from the excessive dearness of many of the articles."

Cape of Good Hope

Cape Town (Rack)

Cape of Good Hope

While in port most of the officers found lodgings ashore, and a small group climbed the mountain country behind the town. On the ships, life continued as usual, with one notable exception: the provision of fresh meat and vegetables for everyone, including the convicts.

Cape Town was the last link with home, and the prospect of departure caused David Collins to reflect sadly:

"The land behind us was the abode of a civilized people; that before us was the residence of savages. When, if ever, we might again enjoy the commerce of the world, was doubtful and uncertain. The refreshments and the pleasures of which we had so liberally partaken at the Cape, were to be exchanged for coarse fare and hard labour at New South Wales. All communication with families and friends now cut off, we were leaving the world behind us, to enter on a state unknown ..."

On 12 November the Fleet set sail for Botany Bay. Several days later Phillip outlined his plan to split the Fleet: he would proceed ahead on the *Supply*, with the hope of gaining sufficient time to survey the Botany Bay area and determine the most appropriate place for the settlement before the arrival of the main convoy. The three fastest transports, the *Alexander*, *Scarborough* and *Friendship* would also travel on ahead. The rest of the Fleet would follow more slowly, under Captain Hunter's command. The Fleet was duly separated on 25 November, and the final phase of the long journey began.

View of Table Mountain from the bay (Raper)

Cape Town (Rack)

Arrival

From Cape Town across the Indian Ocean to Botany Bay, the divided Fleet was at sea for eight weeks. Christmas Day was celebrated with traditional fare:

"Dinned off a pice of pork & apple Sauce a pice of Beef & plum pudding, and Crowned the Day With 4 Bottels of Rum ..."

crowed James Scott. Chaplain Richard Johnson recorded that on the *Golden Grove* a similar meal was consumed with difficulty: *"our plates, &c., tumbling down, and we scarcely able to keep upon our seats."* Rough seas continued to toss the ships, and a week later Bowes Smyth wrote that *"many of the Women were wash'd out of their Births by the Seas we ship'd."*

As the weather became warmer, the plants obtained en route bloomed in Bowes Smyth's cabin:

"There are now in the Cabin Geraniums in full blossum & some Grape Vines wh. flourish very much, there are also Myrtles, Bananas & several other sorts of plants brot. from Rio de Janeiro."

Van Diemen's Land was sighted by the main convoy on 7 January, and at night Collins

"... perceived several fires lighted on the coast, at many of which, no doubt, were some of the native inhabitants, to whom it was probable our novel appearance must have afforded matter of curiosity and wonder."

Encounter with Aborigines (Bradley)

The *Supply* reached Botany Bay on 18 January. Phillip's plan *"to fix on the situation most eligible for the colony, before the transports should arrive"* came to naught: the *Alexander*, *Scarborough* and *Friendship* anchored in Botany Bay on 19 January; followed the next day by the *Sirius* with the rest of the convoy.

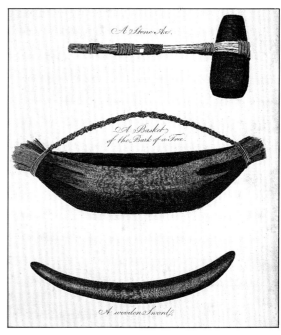

Axe, basket and throwing stick

Arrival

Exploration of Botany Bay was a high priority, leading almost immediately to encounters with local Aborigines.

Phillip wished from the outset to establish good relations with the Aborigines, evidenced in the first contact between the officials of the First Fleet and the people they dispossessed. The scene was recorded by Philip Gidley King, one of the participants:

"... we put the Boats onshore near where we observed two of their Canoes lying, they immediately got up & called to us in a Menacing tone, & at the same time brandishing their spears or lances, however the Governor shewed them some beads & orderd a Man to fasten them to the stem of the Canoe, we then made signs that we wanted Water, when they pointed round the point on which they stood & invited us to land there; on landing they directed us by pointing, to a very fine stream of fresh water, Governor Phillip then advanced toward them alone & unarmed, on which one of them advanced towards him, but would not come near enough to receive the beads which the Governor held out for him, but seemed very desirous of having them & made signs for them to be lain on ye ground, which was done, he (ye Native) came on with fear & trembling & took them up, & by degrees came so near as to receive Looking Glasses &c, & seemed quite astonished at ye figure we cut in being cloathed & I think it is very easy to conceive ye ridiculous figure we must appear to those poor creatures who were perfectly naked ..."

Aboriginal family at Port Jackson (Freycinet)

The sex of the white men perplexed the Aborigines, a matter dealt with matter-of-factly by King:

"As they took us for women, not having our beards grown, I order one of the people to undecieve them in this particular ..."

Several day later, Watkin Tench, accompanied by a seven year-old child, had a similarly cautious encounter, terminated by the local people:

"After nearly an hour's conversation by signs and gestures, they repeated several times the word whurra, which signifies, begone, and walked away from us to the head of the Bay."

A view of Botany Bay

Arrival

On closer inspection, the grasslands described by Cook's party proved a chimera. The soil was considered unsuitable for cultivation, the water supply inadequate, the wood unsuitable for building purposes, and the bay itself exposed to heavy seas.

Leaving instructions that the land near Port Sutherland be cleared for possible settlement, Phillip set off to explore alternative sites. His party headed north to Port Jackson, taking three longboats. In words which are now famous, he later wrote to Lord Sydney describing the place he selected for the new colony:

"We got into Port Jackson early in the Afternoon, and had the satisfaction of finding the finest Harbour in the World, in which a thousand sail of the line may ride in the most perfect security...

The different Coves were examined with all possible expedition: I fixed on the one that had the best spring of Water and in which the Ships can Anchor so close to the Shore that at a very small expence Quays may be made at which the largest Ships may unload.

This Cove, which I honoured with the Name of Sydney, is about a quarter of a Mile across at the entrance, and half a Mile in length."

The day after Phillip's return to Botany Bay, *"the greatest astonishment was spread through the fleet by the appearance of two ships, under French colours."* These were correctly surmised by Phillip to be a French expedition on a voyage of discovery, under the command of La Pérouse. Winds and currents prevented closer contact, and the two French ships disappeared south of the Bay.

'Natives of Botany Bay'

View in Broken Bay (Bradley)

Arrival

On 25 January Phillip sailed to Port Jackson in the *Supply*. The rest of the Fleet was ordered to follow as soon as the strong wind abated. Before they were able to make their way out of Botany Bay, however, the French ships reappeared and civilities were exchanged.

Phillip's wish for a speedy removal to Port Jackson caused the Fleet considerable trouble, as Bowes Smyth described:

"The Charlotte was once in the most imminent danger of being on the Rocks–The Friendship & Prince of Wales who cd. not keep in stays came foul of each other & the Friendship carried away her Jib Boom–The Prince of Wales had her New Main-sail & Main topmast staysail rent in pieces by the Friendships yd... however at last the whole fleet got clear of the Harbour's mouth without any further damage being sustain'd, Every one blaming the Rashness of the Governor in insisting upon the fleets workg. out in such weather, & all agreed it was next to a Miracle that some of the Ships were not lost, the danger was so very great."

Meanwhile in Sydney Cove, a party was sent ashore early in the morning to clear the ground near the fresh water stream. The wading birds depicted on the stamp are white cranes, noticed by Bowes Smyth *"standg. on the mud by the side of the water at least 5 ft. high."* Behind the cranes are yellow gum plants, with long central shoots used by Aborigines to make spears.

'Yellow gum plant'

Sydney Cove (Watling)

Arrival

By nightfall on 26 January the whole of the convoy was safely anchored in Sydney Cove. The final stamp in the First Fleet series is based on the well-known painting by Algernon Talmage, depicting the scene described in the official account:

"In the evening of the 26th the colours were displayed on shore, and the Governor, with several of his principal officers and others, assembled round the flag-staff, drank the king's health, and success to the settlement ..."

Establishment of the settlement began in earnest the next day, with the landing of a detachment of marines and some of the male convicts. Land was cleared, tents pitched and stores unloaded. On the east side of the cove, near the stream, a portable canvas house was erected for the Governor. Nearby were tents for a group of female convicts. The other convicts were put on the western side, with the marine encampment. Hospital tents were soon required. Although comparatively little illness was recorded during the voyage, outbreaks of both dysentery and scurvy occurred soon after landing.

A second ceremony was held on 7 February, in the presence of the whole colony: convicts, marines and officials. David Collins, the Deputy Judge Advocate, read aloud the Royal Commission appointing Arthur Phillip the Captain General and Governor in Chief of the territory of New South Wales, together with the letters patent for establishing civil and criminal courts. Governor Phillip then addressed the gathering, thanking the marines for their *"steady good conduct on every occasion."* The convicts were warned of the consequences of disobeying the law, an exhortation thought to have been prompted, at least in part, by *"the scene of debauchery and riot"* following the landing of the women convicts. Those who did not work would not eat. Conversely, the governor *"should ever be ready to shew approbation and encouragement to those who proved themselves worthy of them by good conduct and attention to orders."*

Thus the guidelines for the colony were set, based, as Phillip's biographer, Alan Frost, has pointed out, on the principles of material comfort, equality and opportunity, rather than on birth and inherited wealth or power. This outcome lay far ahead, however. George Worgan, the *Sirius* surgeon who included a piano among his accoutrement for the voyage, summed up the immediate prospect:

"I thought the Governor, spoke with a Feeling and a Concern, that does Honour to his Humanity, and it is really a Pity, he has the Government of a set of Reprobates who will not suffer him to indulge himself in a Lenity, which he sincerely wishes to govern them by."

The events of the early years of settlement and the fate of those reprobates are the subject of the last book of this series.

'The Founding of Australia' (Talmage)

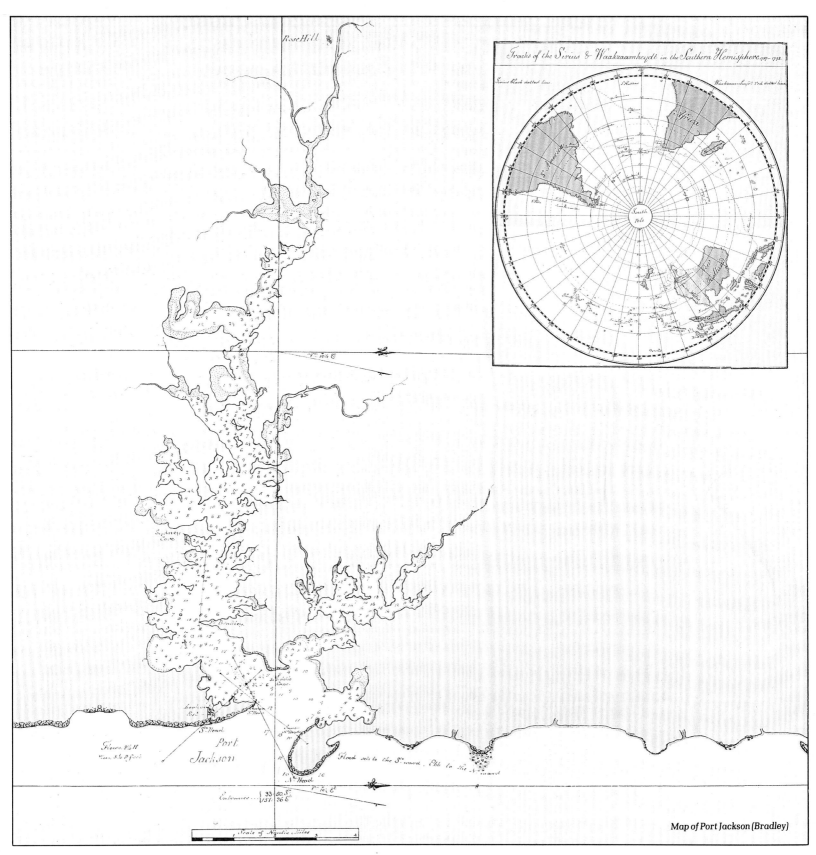

Map of Port Jackson (Bradley)

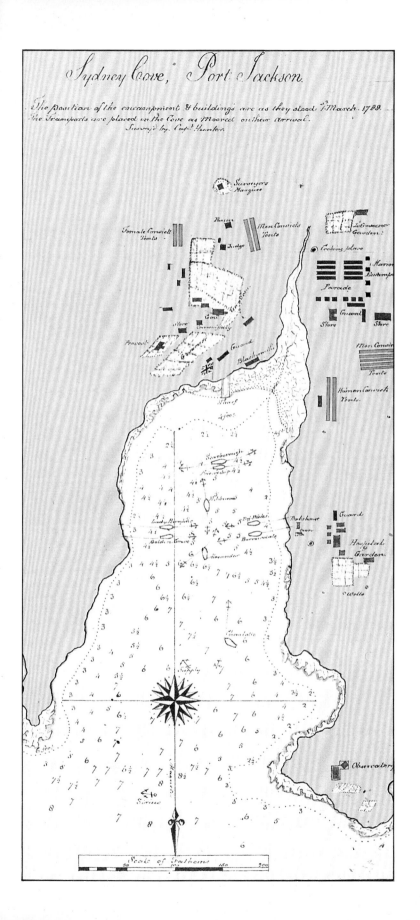

Map of Sydney Cove, Port Jackson (Bradley)

BIBLIOGRAPHY
General

Bateson, Charles. *The Convict Ships 1787-1868*. 2nd edn. Sydney, Reed, 1974. 1st pub. 1959.

Cobley, John. *The Crimes of the First Fleet Convicts*. Sydney, Angus & Robertson, 1970.

Crittenden, Victor. *A Bibliography of the First Fleet*. Canberra, Australian National University Press, 1981.

Crittenden, Victor. *The Voyage of the First Fleet 1787 - 1788*. Canberra, Mulini Press, 1981.

Fidlon, Paul G. & Ryan, R.J. *The First Fleeters. A Comprehensive Listing of Convicts, Marines, Seamen, Officers, Wives, Children and Ships*. Sydney, Australian Documents Library, 1981.

Frost, Alan. *Arthur Phillip 1738-1814: His Voyaging*. Melbourne, Oxford University Press, 1987.

Heney, Helen. *Australia's Founding Mothers*. Melbourne, Nelson, 1978.

King, Jonathan. *The First Fleet: The Convict Voyage that Founded Australia 1787-88*. Melbourne, Macmillan, 1982.

O'Brien, Eris. *The Foundation of Australia (1786-1800)*. 2nd edn. Sydney, Angus & Robertson, 1950. 1st pub. 1937.

First Fleet Narratives

(For a comprehensive list, see Crittenden's *A Bibliography of the First Fleet*)

Bradley, William. *A Voyage to New South Wales: The Journal of Lieutenant William Bradley RN of HMS Sirius 1786-1792*. Sydney, The Trustees of the Public Library of New South Wales in association with Ure Smith, 1969.

Collins, David. *An Account of the English Colony in New South Wales*, edited by B. H. Fletcher. Sydney, Reed in association with the Royal Australian Historical Society, 1975. 2v. 1st pub. 1798.

Easty, John. *Memorandum of the Transactions of a Voyage from England to Botany Bay 1787-1793*. Sydney, The Trustees of the Public Library of New South Wales in association with Angus & Robertson, 1965.

King, Philip Gidley. *The Journal of Philip Gidley King: Lieutenant, RN 1787-1790*, edited by P. G. Fidlon and R. J. Ryan. Sydney, Australian Documents Library, 1980.

[Phillip, Arthur] *The Voyage of Governor Phillip to Botany Bay*, edited by J. J. Auchmuty. Sydney, Angus & Robertson in association with the Royal Australian Historical Society, 1970. 1st pub. 1789.

Scott, James. *Remarks on a Passage to Botany Bay 1787-1792*. Sydney, The Trustees of the Public Library of New South Wales in association with Angus & Robertson, 1963.

Smyth, Arthur Bowes. *The Journal of Arthur Bowes Smyth: Surgeon, Lady Penrhyn 1787-1789*, edited by P. G. Fidlon and R. J. Ryan. Sydney, Australian Documents Library, 1979.

Tench, Watkin. *Sydney's First Four Years*, edited by L. F. Fitzhardinge. Sydney, Angus & Robertson in association with the Royal Australian Historical Society, 1961. 1st pub. in two parts: *A Narrative of the Expedition to Botany Bay* (1789) and *A Complete Account of the Settlement at Port Jackson* (1793).

White, John. *Journal of a Voyage to New South Wales*, edited by A. H. Chisholm. Sydney, Angus & Robertson in association with the Royal Australian Historical Society, 1962. 1st pub. 1790.

Worgan, George. *Journal of a First Fleet Surgeon*. Sydney, the Library Council of New South Wales in association with the Library of Australian History, 1978.

ACKNOWLEDGEMENTS

Sue Passmore's illustrations for the First Fleet stamps are based upon the original paintings and journals of people aboard First Fleet ships, together with reference material gathered from repositories in Australia and overseas. Expert advice has been provided by a number of people: most particularly, the ships were vetted by Mr Karl Marquardt, a maritime historian and artist, curators of the National Gallery of Victoria assisted with costume details, curators of the Australian War Memorial checked the uniforms, and curators and staff of the Museum of Victoria were consulted concerning the wildlife observed en route and the portrayal of the Aborigines of New South Wales.

Australia Post warmly thanks Mr Marquardt and the staff of the institutions for their co-operation and assistance. Thanks are also due to Dr. L. L. Robson, Reader in History, University of Melbourne, for his assistance during preparation of the text. Photographs, paintings, drawings and maps have been reproduced with kind permission from the following:

BBC Hulton Picture Library, London: p.29 Refreshment after lunch on the Place du Palais, & p.31 Religious procession in Rio de Janeiro, both in *Voyage Pittoresque à Bresil*, by Jean Baptiste Debret.

Bridgeman Art Library, London: p.9 Portsmouth Point, by Thomas Rowlandson.

British Library, London: p.21 Peak of Teneriffe and town of Santa Cruz, 1792; p.25 Sketch of the Harbour and City of Rio de Janeiro (map) 1792/3; p.27 View in Rio de Janeiro, by Sydney Parkinson, 1768/69; p.35 Table Bay and Cape Colony, map by Captain G. Bridges, early 1790s.

British Museum (Natural History), London: five paintings by George Raper: p.4-5 Entrance of Rio de Janeiro, 1790; p.7 & p.39 View of the Table-land from the anchorage in the bay, Cape of Good Hope, 1792; p.15 *Supply* and *Sirius*; p.17 View of the Needles, 1789; p.33 Cobras, a fortified island close to the City in Rio de Janeiro, 1789; p.47 A partial view of Sydney Cove taken from the sea side before the Surgeon General's house, by Thomas Watling.

Marion Fletcher: p.11 Fashion plate from the *Gallery of Fashion* (English), reproduced in *Costume in Australia, 1788-1901* by Marion Fletcher. Melbourne, Oxford University Press, 1984.

Guildhall Library, London: p.9 The Convicts taking Water near Black Friars Bridge, in order for their being conveyed to Woolwich, & p.13 View of the Justitia Hulk, with the Convicts at Work, near Woolwich, both in *The Malefactor's Register; or the Newgate and Tyburn Calendar, etc.* London, Alexander Hogg, c.1779.

La Trobe Collection, State Library of Victoria: p.41 A Stone Axe, A Basket of the Bark of a Tree, A Wooden Sword, p.45 Natives of Botany Bay, & p.47 Yellow Gum Plant, all in *The Voyage of Governor Phillip to Botany Bay*. London, John Stockdale, 1790. p.43 Nouvelle-Hollande Famille de Sauvages, in *Voyage Autour du Monde*, by Louis-Claude Freycinet. Paris, 1825.

Mansell Collection, London: p.37 Town Hall, Cape of Good Hope, by Johannes Rack, 1764; p.39 Parade and Heeregracht, Cape of Good Hope, by Johannes Rack, 1763; p.43 A view of Botany Bay, in *The Voyage of Governor Phillip to Botany Bay*.

Karl Marquardt: p.25 Landfall at Van Diemen's land 5.1.1788, H.M. Brig Supply, & p.35 Daybreak 13.5.1787, We are sailing, both by Karl Marquardt.

Melhoramentos de São Paulo: p.29 O negro trovador, and Vendedoras de aluá, & p.31 Cena de rua do Rio de Janeiro, all in *Viagem Pitoresca e Histórica ao Brasil* by Jean Baptiste Debret. São Paulo, Edicões Melhoramentos, 1971.

Mitchell Library, State Library of New South Wales: p.6 Arthur Phillip by Francis Wheatley, Philip Gidley King unknown artist, John Hunter by W. M. Bennett, David Collins by I. T. Barber (owned by Miss Anne Trelawney), & Watkin Tench unknown artist (owned by The Misses Grylls); 10 paintings and maps by William Bradley: p.17 *Sirius, Supply* & Convoy: Needle Point ENE 3 miles. *Hyena* in company, 13 May 1787; p.19 *Sirius* track from England to the Equator showing Teneriffe, map; p.23 Santa Cruz on the SE side of Teneriffe: *Sirius* & Convoy in the Roads, June 1787; p.27 Fortified Bay on the West side the Entrance of Rio Janeiro (sic), Coast of Brazil; p.33 City of St Sebastians, Rio Janeiro (sic); p.41 First Interview with the Native Women at Port Jackson, New South Wales; p.45 View in Broken Bay, New South Wales, March 1788; p.50 Tracks of *Sirius* and *Waakzaamheydt* in the Southern Hemisphere 1787-1792, map, & Map of Port Jackson; p.51 Map of Sydney Cove, Port Jackson.

National Library of Australia: p.6 Convicts embarking for Botany Bay, by Thomas Rowlandson.

National Maritime Museum, London: p.2-3 & p.13 A Geometrical Plan of His Majesty's Dock-Yard at Deptford, 1753; p.7 Admiralty plan of HMS *Supply* & A Plan of His Majesty's Dock Yard at Portsmouth, 1774; p.11 A Gig's Crew, by J. A. Atkinson, 1808; p.13 Two Seamen, by J. A. Atkinson, 1808; p.15 Deptford Docks, by John Cleveley the elder, 1757; p.21 Santa Cruz in the Island of Teneriffe, 1791; p.23 Santa Croix de Ténériffe, n.d.; p.37 Cape of Good Hope, 1794.

National Portrait Gallery, London: front cover: Arthur Phillip, by Francis Wheatley, 1786.

Tate Gallery, London: p.49 The Founding of Australia, by Algernon Talmage, 1937.